CHINA

Stephen Keeler

Franklin Watts

New York/Chicago/London/Toronto/Sydney

Copyright © 1987, 1994 Franklin Watts

Franklin Watts
95 Madison Avenue
New York, NY 10016

Library of Congress Cataloging-in-Publication Data

Keeler, Stephen.
    Passport to China/Stephen Keeler.
        p.   cm. – (Passport to)
    Includes index.
    ISBN 0-531-14320-1
    1. China – Juvenile literature.   [1. China.]   I. Title   II. Series.
DS706.K44   1993
951.05'8 – dc20   93-38982
                                                                        CIP AC

Editor: Lynne Williams
Design: Edward Kinsey
Illustrations: Hayward Art Group
Consultant: Keith Lye

Photographs: Richard and Sally Greenhill,
Stephen Keeler, Edward Kinsey,
Chris Fairclough, Kate Mulvey,
British Petroleum, Gamma, Panos Pictures,
Popperfoto, Frank Spooner Pictures, Zefa

Front cover: Julia Waterlow

Printed in Belgium

Contents

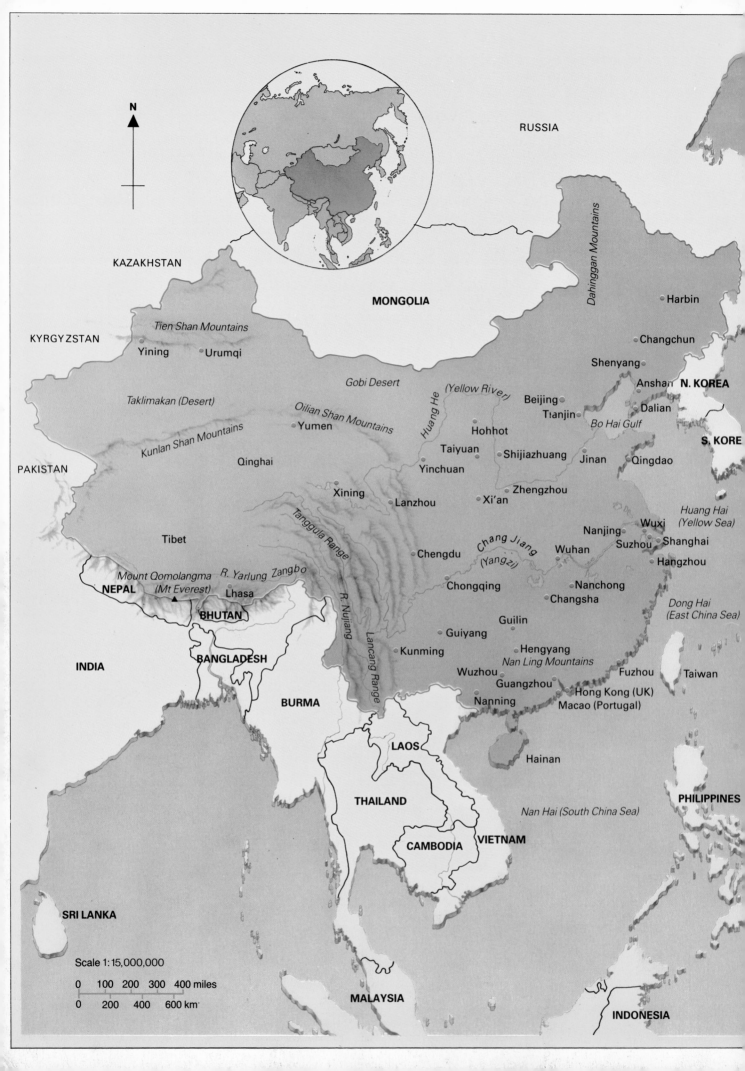

N

KAZAKHSTAN

KYRGYZSTAN

RUSSIA

MONGOLIA

Dahinggan Mountains

• Harbin

• Changchun

Shenyang •

Tien Shan Mountains

Yining •   • Urumqi

Gobi Desert

Huang He *(Yellow River)*

Anshan •   **N. KOREA**

Beijing •   • Dalian

Taklimakan (Desert)

Tıanjin •

Qilian Shan Mountains

• Yumen

Hohhot •

Taiyuan •

Bo Hai Gulf

S. KORE

Kunlan Shan Mountains

Qinghai

Shijiazhuang •   Jinan •   • Qingdao

Yinchuan •

PAKISTAN

• Xining

Lanzhou •

Xi'an •

Zhengzhou •

*Huang Hai
(Yellow Sea)*

Tanggula Range

Nanjing •   Wuxi •

Wuhan •   Suzhou • • Shanghai

Tibet

Chang Jiang
(Yangzi)

Chengdu •

Hangzhou •

R. Yarlung Zangbo

Mount Qomolangma
(Mt Everest)

NEPAL

Lhasa •

Chongqing •

Nanchong •

Changsha •

*Dong Hai
(East China Sea)*

BHUTAN

R. Nujiang

Guilin •

BANGLADESH

Guiyang •

Hengyang •

INDIA

Lancang Range

Kunming •

Nan Ling Mountains

Fuzhou •

Wuzhou •

• Taiwan

BURMA

Guangzhou •

Nanning •

Hong Kong (UK)

Macao (Portugal)

LAOS

Hainan

THAILAND

PHILIPPINES

Nan Hai (South China Sea)

CAMBODIA   **VIETNAM**

SRI LANKA

Scale 1:15,000,000

0   100 200 300 400 miles

0   200   400   600 km

MALAYSIA

INDONESIA

Introduction

China is the world's third largest country after Russia and Canada. China is also the world's oldest surviving civilization, with a recorded history going back more than 4,000 years. Paper, printing, money, fireworks, sunglasses and silk are all Chinese inventions, and yet we know less about modern China than about almost any other country.

Although now a major world power, China is also a relatively poor, developing country. Feeding the massive population remains a priority. The government encourages married couples to have only one child.

China has always been a rather closed society. The government is, however, now beginning to open the country to foreign ideas and assistance. China seems ready to take its place in the modern world. Its athletes and musicians are taking part in international events. More young people are sent overseas for training and China now welcomes thousands of foreign tourists each year, curious to get a glimpse of life behing the "bamboo curtain."

Above: Villagers on their way to and from the weekly market near Xin Ping, in Yunnan Province.

Below: Nanjing Lu is Central Shanghai's best-stocked and busiest shopping street.

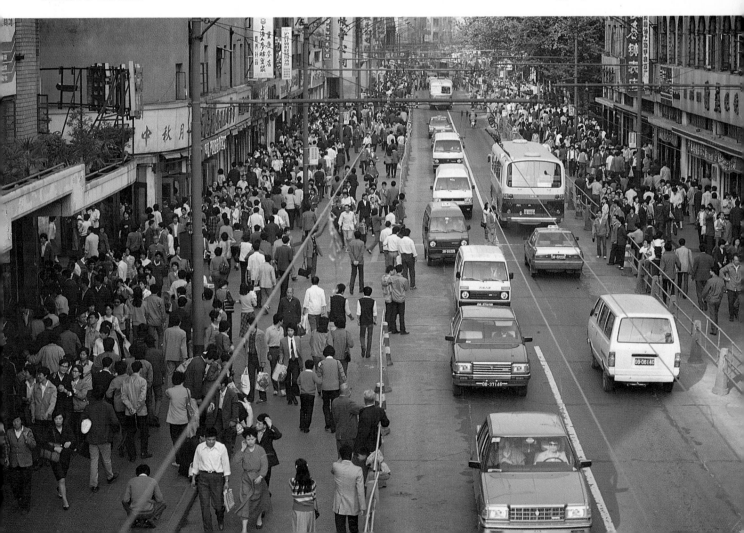

The land

China shares its 14,160-mile (22,800-km) border with 14 countries. China is about the same size as all the countries of Europe put together. Nearly three-fifths of the country is mountain, desert and water.

The country can be broadly divided into five geographical regions. The North China Plain, northeast of the capital Beijing (Peking), is surrounded on three sides by mountains. It is an important wheat-producing area, but winter temperatures can fall as low as –40°F (–40°C).

The Inner Mongolian Plateau, in the north and northwest, has very little vegetation apart from grass. Nomadic Mongols and Tibetans have raised flocks of sheep and goats here for thousands of years. Strong Siberian winds – freezing in winter but scorching in summer – carry clouds of soft, yellow dust, called *loess*, from the Gobi Desert to Beijing and beyond. Hundreds of millions of trees have been planted in north and northwest China in an attempt to stop the damaging soil erosion caused by these winds.

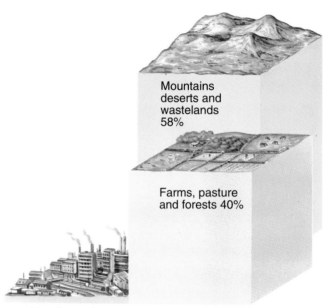

Mountains deserts and wastelands 58%

Farms, pasture and forests 40%

Housing and industry 2%

Above: China's biggest problem is how to feed its huge population as only some of its land can be cultivated.

Below: Rice, the principal crop of southern China, is grown in flooded "fields" called paddies, like these near the Macao border.

The soft, rich, yellow loess soil blown in from the northern deserts and carried down by the Huang (Yellow) River has made central China an agriculturally rich area. It produces much of the country's wheat, millet, cotton, rice and tea. Around 300 million people live in this region.

The Qinghai-Tibet Plateau is the largest highland region in the world. It covers more than 772,200 sq miles (2 million sq km) of western China and stretches to the Himalayas in the south. Both the climate and the geography are inhospitable and the population averages only nine inhabitants per sq mile (3 per sq km) in this remote part of "the roof of the world."

The tropical climate of southern China makes it possible to bring in three harvests each year. Mountains protect the region from cold northwesterly winds. The city of Kunming is known as the "city of eternal spring," even though it is 6,200 feet (1,890 m) above sea level.

Above: This dramatic mountain scenery can be seen along the banks of the Li Jiang river near Guilin, in Guanxi Province.

Below: In Tibet, much of the flat, open grassland is surrounded by high mountain ranges and peaks.

The people

Although 94 percent of the people of China are Han Chinese, the remaining 6 percent, or approximately 91 million people, belong to one of 56 ethnic minority nationalities. These minorities live in half of China's territory and in all the border regions of Inner Mongolia, Xinjiang, Tibet and the provinces of Yunnan, Guizhou, Guangdong and the autonomous region of Guangxi.

The largest ethnic minority groups include the Zhuang (12.5 million), the Manchu (7.9 million), the Hui (6 million), and the Tibetans (2.2 million). They have their own languages and religions. Many are Buddhists, some are Muslims and there are some Christians. These groups have special rights and privileges in modern China. All ethnic minority children have the right to study their own language at school – and of course they also have to learn Chinese. Some areas, such as Inner Mongolia, Tibet, and Xinjiang, are called Autonomous Regions and have limited freedom from the central government in Beijing.

Above: The children of ship workers at a kindergarten in Guangzhou (more commonly known as Canton).

Below: These villagers, with Chinese Han features, live near Xi'an in Shaanxi Province.

Above: Li Bao-Chen is a retired farm worker.

Below: A Miao woman from Kunming.

Above: Tibetans from Qinghai Province.

Below: Soldiers of the People's Liberation Army.

Although China is not a rich country, it is developing rapidly. It is modernizing and expanding its industry and scientific research. Great improvements have been made in housing, transportation and education. People are living longer and earning more than ever. All this would be lost if the population growth is not halted.

In order to encourage couples to have only one child, the Chinese government offers generous cash grants and other benefits such as improved housing. These are withdrawn and must be repaid, in some cases, if a second child is born.

In China loyalty and comradeship are highly valued. People are expected to be considerate and polite. They work hard and have a strong sense of responsibility to their local communities, to the country as a whole, and to its leaders. Old people are especially respected. Their views and advice are always taken very seriously. The Chinese are proud of their history and confident about the future.

Above: Road workers in Guangdong Province.

Below: Birth control posters in Beijing.

Where people live

About 25 percent of the world's population lives in China, on only 6.4 percent of the earth's land surface. More people live in China than in any country on earth. Within China, over 80 percent of the population lives in the eastern and southeastern regions, on less than a fifth of China's total land area.

There are more than 3,500 towns and cities, and twelve of these have populations of more than two million. In the 1970s and 1980s, the proportion of people in urban areas has been increasing rapidly, but 67 percent still live in rural areas. Most of them work on the land.

Shanghai is the largest city in China. Including its suburbs, it contains more than 13 million people. It is a bustling, attractive place and its people are thought to be among the most modern and fashionable in China. Many young people would like to move from the countryside to such cities as Shanghai or Guangzhou (Canton), but these cities are already overcrowded and suffer from pollution.

Above: Women in traditional costume in Yunnan Province.

Below: A riverside settlement near Yangshan in southwest China.

Left: Shanghai's waterfront architecture is a reminder of the days of European domination of the city.

Below: The magnificent Potala Palace, former residence of the Dalai Lama. It is in Lhasa, capital of Tibet, which is now an Autonomous Region of China.

Between 1949 and the late 1970s, people's rights to move around the country and change jobs were very restricted. People belonged to "work units" where they lived, went to school and eventually worked. But from the 1970s, the creation of special economic zones in eastern China led to a rapid expansion of industrial activity. These zones attracted millions of people from the poorer rural areas where there was often not enough work to employ them.

Agriculture was organized in cooperative teams until the late 1970s, when the government agreed that the cooperatives could be divided up and farmed by families. This was part of the "Four Modernizations" policy. It led to a rapid expansion of farm production, although the farmers still sold part of their output to the government and part in "free markets."

In the past, China's peasants suffered extreme hardship and poverty. Today, more efficient central control over agriculture and increasing free enterprise help to create many wealthy peasant farmers throughout China.

Beijing

Beijing, or Peking as it is often known in English, is unlike any other major capital city in the world. It is the largest city in China, covering an area of 6,564 sq miles (17,000 sq km). It has the second largest population, after Shanghai. It has existed for more than 3,000 years and has been a capital city, on and off, for over 800 years. Yet in Beijing today, little remains of the city's splendid past.

About 500 years ago Beijing contained four walled cities. At the center was The Forbidden City with its magnificent palaces, where the emperor lived and ruled. No building was allowed to be constructed that could overlook its formidable walls, and ordinary citizens were forbidden from entering. Over the centuries successive invading armies damaged and destroyed large sections of Beijing and its city walls, which were never restored. In more recent years, walls and gateways have been demolished to make way for new highways, factories and housing.

Above: The Great Wall of China snakes across the hillsides at Badaling Pass, near Beijing.

Below: Some of the best known landmarks to have survived Beijing's turbulent history.

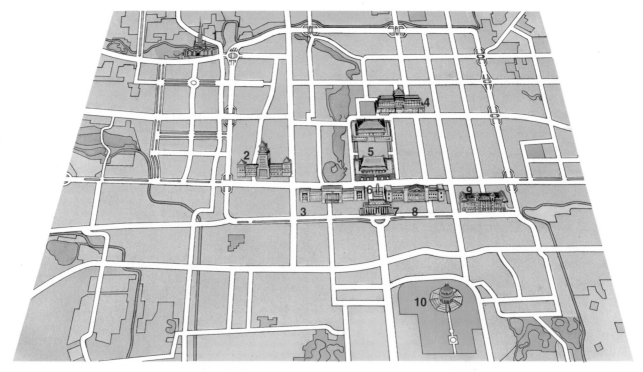

1 Exhibition Center
2 Cultural Palace of the Nationalities
3 Great Hall of the People
4 National Art Gallery
5 Palace Museum (Forbidden City)
6 Tiananmen (Gate of Heavenly Peace)
7 Mao Zedong Mausoleum
8 Museum of the Chinese Revolution
9 Railway Station
10 Temple of Heaven

The Forbidden City, now renamed The Palace Museum, survived and today is Beijing's biggest tourist attraction.

The main entrance is Tiananmen (Gate of Heavenly Peace), which stands on the northern edge of Tiananmen Square, the largest public square in the world. At the southern end of Tiananmen Square is the mausoleum, which houses the embalmed body of China's first Communist leader, Chairman Mao Zedong, who died in 1976.

To the southeast is one of the architectural wonders of the world – The Tian Tan or Temple of Heaven. This is a collection of buildings set in beautiful parkland. The largest building is the Hall of Prayer for Good Harvests which is over 450 years old. It was built entirely of wood without the use of nails, screws or cement.

The Great Wall of China passes within 50 miles (80 km) of Beijing. Built as a defense against northern invaders, work started on it more than 2,500 years ago. Today it is 3,946 miles (6,350 km) long.

Above: Tiananmen, the Gate of Heavenly Peace.

Below: The Hall of Prayer for Good Harvests, Temple of Heaven.

Fact file : land and population

Key facts

Location: China is situated in the eastern and southeastern part of the Asian continent, on the west coast of the Pacific Ocean. Mainland China lies between latitudes 21° North and 54° North and longitudes 75° East and 135° East.

Main parts: Mainland China is divided into 22 provinces, 5 autonomous regions and 3 centrally administered municipalities. Taiwan is the largest of over 5,000 Chinese islands, but China's claim to sovereignty over Taiwan is not recognized internationally. Hong Kong, a British colony on the coast of China, will be returned to Chinese rule on July 1, 1977. The nearby Portuguese territory of Macao will be returned to China in 1999.

Area: 3,691,502 sq miles (9,560,925 sq km).

Population: 1,151,486,000 (1991 estimate). Other areas: Hong Kong (pop 5,693,000); Macao (399,000); and Taiwan (20,658,000).

Capital: Beijing (Peking).

Major cities:
Shanghai (7,780,000; city and suburbs 12,760,000)
Beijing (5,762,000; city and suburbs 10,860,000)
Tianjin (4,850,000)
Shenyang (4,289,000)
Wuhan (3,200,000)

Main languages: Putong Hua ("Mandarin" Chinese) (official). Other Chinese dialects include Yue (Cantonese), Wu, Xiang, Hui and Hakka.

Highest point: Mount Qomolangma (Mount Everest) 29,028 ft (8,848 m).

Longest rivers: Chang Jiang (Yangzi) 3,915 miles (6,300 km), Huang He (Yellow) 3,395 miles (5,464 km).

Largest lake: Qinghai Lake (saltwater) 1,660 sq miles (4,300 sq km).

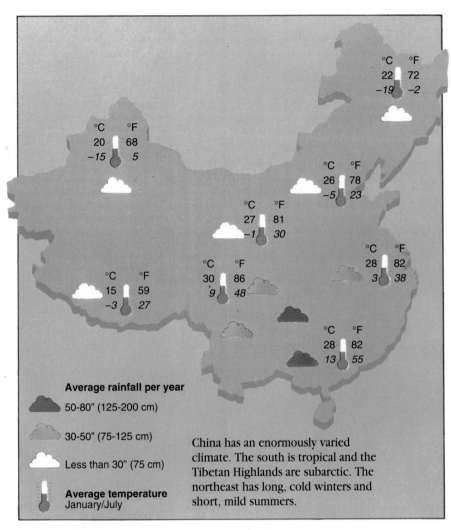

Average rainfall per year

50-80" (125-200 cm)

30-50" (75-125 cm)

Less than 30" (75 cm)

Average temperature
January/July

China has an enormously varied climate. The south is tropical and the Tibetan Highlands are subarctic. The northeast has long, cold winters and short, mild summers.

CHINA

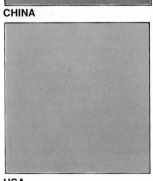

USA

AUSTRALIA

FRANCE

GREAT
BRITAIN

△ **A land area comparison**
China's land area of 3,691,462 sq miles (9,560,900 sq km) is the third largest in the world. The United States has 3,600,000 sq miles (9,370,000 sq km), Australia has 2,470,000 sq miles (7,650,000 sq km), and Britain a mere 88,795 sq miles (229,070 sq km).

China   311 per sq mile
(120 per sq km)

Australia   5 per sq mile
(2 per sq km)

USA   70 per sq mile
(27 per sq km)

Britain   614 per sq mile
(237 per sq km)

△ **A population density comparison**
Few countries have such an uneven
distribution of population as China. In
Shanghai, for example, there are 5,200
people per sq mile (2,000 per sq km)
while in all Tibet there are only 3.9
people per sq mile (1.5 per sq km).

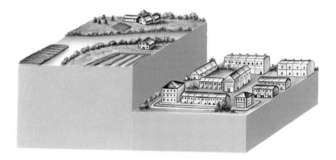

Country   67%   Cities and towns   33%

△ **Where people live**
In 1965, 82 percent of the
population of China lived in rural
areas. Today, more and more
people are living in cities and
towns.

△ **Major population centers**
China has twelve cities with more
than 2,000,000 inhabitants. The
population is concentrated in the
eastern part of the country.

Harbin

Urumqi

Shenyang

Beijing

Tianjin

Xining   Lanzhou

X'ian

Nanjing

Shanghai

Lhasa

Chengdu

Chongoing

Wuhan

Kunming

Guangzhou

🏠 Major Cities
— Railways

Home life

Like almost everything else in China home life varies greatly between the towns and the countryside. Despite a rapid movement of people to the cities, two out of every three Chinese remain peasants who work on the land. Their small houses are usually built from mud or clay bricks and have thatched or tiled roofs. Many have no electricity or running water.

Charcoal stoves provide much of the home's heating. Beds made of bamboo mats and padded cotton quilts are often laid on a raised brick platform called a *kang*. A chimney from the stove passes under the *kang* and the hot smoke keeps the bed pleasantly warm.

It is common for three generations – grandparents, parents and children – to live together in these three- or four-room cottages. Grandparents usually look after young children, prepare the family's meals and do much of the lighter housework. Parents work in the fields or with animals or farm machinery. The children usually help with feeding animals, growing and gathering crops and doing housework.

Above: A village in Liaoning, northeast China.
Below: Children playing a reading game.

Below right: Fresh water is supplied to this Dalian village by a communal pump.

Left: Apartments in a Shanghai suburb.

Below: A steelworker and his family in their two-room apartment in Anshan Jilin Province.

Since the government relaxed its strict laws on free enterprise in the early 1980s, peasant families have become much better off. Many have radios – there are over 200 million radios in China – but peasants usually have few personal possessions apart from farm implements and perhaps a shared bicycle.

Families living in the towns and cities are better off than peasants, but they work long hours for low pay and few holidays. Most families live in small houses or apartments owned by their work unit. They usually have electricity and running water. More modern buildings in the colder north may have some form of central heating. Kitchens and toilets are often shared with other families and most work units have separate communal showers or baths for men and women.

Most Chinese rise before dawn and do *taiji* or some other form of exercise, in the street, or in a park, before starting work. They repeat their exercises in the morning break.

Shops and shopping

Most Chinese families do not have refrigerators or freezers. Fresh food, such as meat, fish, bread and some vegetables, has to be bought daily. So for some people shopping occupies a lot of their time each day.

Most urban work units and rural peasant communities have their own shops, so that people do not always have to go to town or the village market each day. These shops supply basic foodstuffs like rice, sugar, tea and cooking oil, as well as some candy and tobacco. They usually sell soap, toothpaste, combs, razor blades and some household goods, such as tools, brooms, buckets, mops and watering cans.

Peasants can now sell their surplus produce freely, often in small "free" markets outside large work units or in city centers. Their fresh eggs, fruit and vegetables are usually of a much higher quality than the food available in the government-run stores and markets, but their prices are very much higher too and not all families can afford to shop there regularly.

Above: Peasant farm workers selling their surplus produce at a "free" market.

Below: These simple but accurate scales are used in markets throughout China.

Below: Imported electronic consumer goods are in big demand but can cost ten times the price of Chinese-made goods.

Grain and cotton products are rationed in China. Work units provide each family with its quota of coupons. There are no major food shortages but deliveries, especially of luxuries or non-essential foods, are sometimes sporadic and never reliable. It is not uncommon to see large crowds in a fruit market if bananas have just arrived.

Large department stores in each town sell everything from ballpoint pens and school exercise books to flashlight batteries, track suits and enamel cups. Clothes are quite cheap but very basic. Chinese silk is beautiful and, by world standards, not expensive. Most of it is produced for export. Throughout China, most people now wear Western-style clothes.

In some towns whole streets are given over to shops selling one type of product. "Bamboo streets" are common, where shops sell mats, blinds, shopping baskets, birdcages, tools, furniture, ornaments and toys, all made from bamboo.

Cooking and eating

The way food is prepared in China and the techniques used to cook it closely reflect the country's geography and the way of life of the people. The northwestern grasslands of Tibet and Qinghai Province are unsuitable for beef and dairy cattle. Beef and other dairy products are therefore not part of the Chinese diet. Protein comes instead from poultry, pigs, and fish, which are easier to raise and cheaper to keep.

Without refrigeration, the Chinese had to develop other ways of preserving food. These include smoking, curing, pickling, salting, crystalizing and drying. In the traditionally large family, someone has always had plenty of time for preparing food. Fuel for cooking has not always been so readily available. So the Chinese "stir-fry" technique has developed. Stir-fried food – usually lots of vegetables with a little meat – is first sliced into dozens of thin strips. This can take a long time, but such thin strips cook quickly in a little oil using a small amount of fuel.

Above: Chinese food is chopped into thin slices before being cooked.

Below: Most dishes contain vegetables and rice. Meat is expensive.

Rice is the staple diet in the south, but northerners eat more bread and noodles made from wheat. They like stews, casseroles and roasts. Delicious Peking duck with its crisp, golden skin and aromatic meat is probably the best-known dish from the north. More fish is eaten in the south. Shark's fin soup is a specialty. Sichuan Province is famous for very hot, spicy food.

Meals for an ordinary family on a normal working day might start with a breakfast of rice porridge with vegetables and a steamed bun. Lunch could be steamed rice, stir-fried vegetables and a thin vegetable soup. Soup usually comes at the end of a meal in China. Supper might be a steamed bun or a bowl of rice porridge. Tea or hot water is usually drunk with meals. The Chinese generally dislike cold food and drink.

On special occasions, such as family weddings, the Chinese often hold lavish banquets with as many as twenty courses.

Above: Outdoor food stalls in Yunnan Province, southwestern China.

Below: Tea being drunk in the shade near Turpan, in the autonomous region of Xinjiang Vighur.

Pastimes and sports

Most Chinese work between 45 and 55 hours a week. They may have up to three weeks' annual vacation, but there are very few public holidays. In their homes they usually have no labor- or time-saving equipment like vacuum cleaners, washing machines or dishwashers. The Chinese, therefore, do not have much leisure time. Nor do they have much money to spend on entertainment or expensive hobbies.

Popular spare time activities include making clothes and slippers, tending the family's vegetable plot, learning a musical instrument and playing cards. Photography is another popular hobby.

People like going to the movies and there is a flourishing Chinese film industry. There are movie theaters in all big towns in China and most work units show feature films about once a month. This is often the social highlight of the month when everyone in the work unit can get together. Films are usually shown at night, outdoors and in all weather. The films are usually semi-political, heroic and have a strong moral message. Foreign films are rarely shown.

Above: Card players in a Shanghai park. Gambling for money is illegal.

Below: A movie theater in downtown Kunming, Yunnan Province.

The extended sickness of a wage-earner can be disastrous for large families. Physical fitness is, therefore, taken very seriously in China and people take part in early-morning exercises in city streets. Most people in the cities practice some form of *wushu* or Chinese martial arts. The young like the rapid, aggressive movements of *kung fu*. The elderly usually prefer the gentler, more graceful *taiji*. For many people, *wushu* is not just a morning exercise, but a serious pursuit involving sword play, costume, and makeup.

The Chinese play basketball and volleyball at school. Nets can be seen strung between posts on dusty open spaces in even the most remote settlements. Badminton is a cheap and practical racket sport and the Chinese are world-famous for their table tennis skills. These are often acquired on communal, concrete "tables" in public parks or the recreation grounds of work units.

Above left: Sword play in Beijing.
Above: In most families children learn to play a musical instrument.

Below: Most of China's best table tennis players learned their early skills in a public park on concrete tables.

News and broadcasting

In 1990, an estimated 27 percent of the population could neither read nor write. In 1964 the figure was 38.1 percent. Yet in 1990 more than 5.6 billion books were printed in China – more than 50 books per head of population. Many of these were political or educational. Bookshops like most other shops in Chinese towns are always crowded. English language textbooks and dictionaries are always among the bestsellers.

The state strictly controls book and newspaper publishing, radio and television broadcasting – all the media. The New China News Agency is the sole source of news. It publishes hundreds of newspapers throughout the country. The most important national paper is *Renmin Ribao*, the *People's Daily*. This is the official newspaper of the central Committee of the Chinese Communist Party. Foreigners living in China can buy *China Daily*, an English language newspaper, but most Chinese people are not normally able to buy foreign newspapers or magazines.

Above: Although daily newspapers can be bought they are also pinned up in public places for all to read, free of charge.

Below: For a small price paperback books can be rented to be read at open-air libraries like this one in southeast China.

Above: A television announcer.

Left: Information and advice about public health, consumer rights, industrial output and local leisure facilities is given in these official wall posters.

Radio and television programs are all made by the Central People's Broadcasting Bureau. Both the New China News Agency and the Central Broadcasting Bureau are under the direct control of the Politburo of the Central Committee of the Communist Party. Both agencies work closely with the Ministries of Education and Culture to coordinate the educational, cultural, artistic and political content of programs.

News, sport and music programs are often broadcast through loudspeakers around work units. The daily, mid-morning physical exercises are done to radio music that is broadcast simultaneously to the whole country.

Color television sets can cost more than an average worker will earn in three years. But many villages share a communal set. Increased prosperity in the 1980s led to an increase in the number of television receivers in circulation. It reached 126 million in 1991.

Below: *Renmin Ribao* (the *People's Daily*) is only one of hundreds of national and local newspapers.

Bottom: Children's books are often based on traditional folktales.

Fact file: home life and leisure

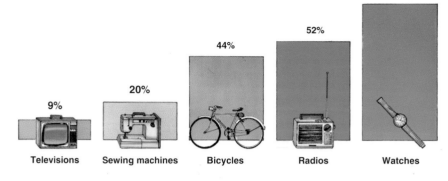

Televisions 9%   Sewing machines 20%   Bicycles 44%   Radios 52%   Watches 91%

Key Facts

Population composition:
People under 15 years of age make up 27.7 percent of the population; a further 30.8 percent are between 15 and 29; people between 30 and 59 make up 32.6 percent; and the remaining 8.9 percent are over 60 years of age.
Average life expectancy at birth: 68 years for men and 72 for women in 1991, as compared with 55 and 59 years respectively in 1965.
Rate of population increase: 1.5 percent per year 1980-91, as compared with 2.2 percent per year in 1965-80. The rate is still falling. It is expected to reach 1.3 percent per year in 1990-2000.
Family life: It is common to find at least three generations of a family sharing the same apartment. The average size of a rural household is 4.9 people, as compared with 3.6 people in urban areas, but these figures are expected to fall.
Homes: People do not own their homes. Housing is provided by work units. Young, single people usually live communally in dormitories. Families usually live in small apartments or houses. Rents are very low.
Work: Hours of work vary greatly between the towns and the countryside. Because most people live at their place of work, average working hours are around 48 hours a week. City dwellers probably work around 9 hours per day, 6 days per week. This often includes a 2-3 hour rest period in the afternoon. Peasants' work is seasonal and usually confined to the hours of daylight.
Religions: There is no state church and religion is not encouraged. However, it is not illegal to practice a religion.

Housing and transport 3%

Food 58%

Other goods and services 4%

Alcohol, tobacco and tea 5%

Entertainment and education 2%

Household goods and services 9%

Clothing and footware 16%

Fuel and power 3%

△ **How many urban households owned goods in the 1980s**
These figures refer mainly to urban households. Families living in the country have few if any consumer goods.

◁ **How the average household budget was spent in the 1980s**
After essential items have been bought there is little left for luxuries or entertainment. This is slowly beginning to change as restrictions are lifted on earnings. There is now a large demand for Japanese color television sets, calculators and cameras.

▽ **Chinese currency and postage stamps**
Chinese currency is called *renminibi*, which means "the people's currency." One *yuan* is divided into ten *jiao* known as "Mao." Each "Mao" is divided into ten *fen*.

Midnight

(clock diagram, reading clockwise from midnight)

Sleep
Breakfast
Exercise
Start school / Start work
Exercise
Work/school
Midday / Lunch
Afternoon nap / shopping
Work/school
Housework
Cookery/homework / Housework
Evening meal
Housework
Leisure

Official public holidays are on New Year's Day (January 1), Labor Day (May 1) and National Days (October 1 and 2). The most popular holiday period is Spring Festival (or Chinese New Year) which is in early February.

▽ **Number of popular leisure pursuits in the 1980s**

At least three times a week

52%	48%	46%
Listening to radio	Physical exercises/ sport	Reading books/ newspapers

At least once a week

55%	52%	32%
Practicing a handicraft	Knitting/ sewing	Learning a skill

At least once a month

49%	88%	9%
Watching TV	Movies	Visiting/ entertaining

◁ **How vacations are spent**
Vacations are a time for families whose members live and work in distant regions of the country to re-unite. Work units and youth organizations arrange visits and camps, especially as a reward for outstanding work. There are very few vacation resorts and no real vacation industry.

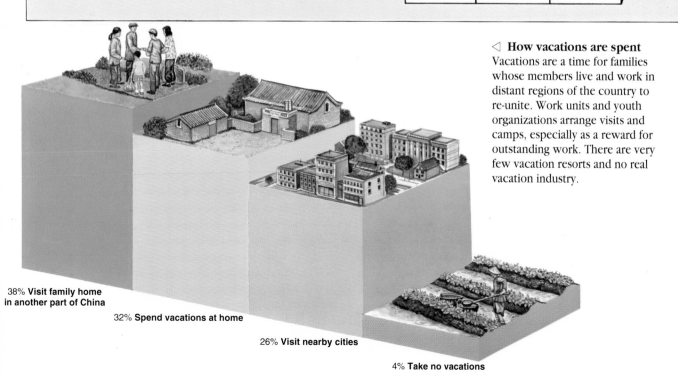

38% **Visit family home in another part of China**

32% **Spend vacations at home**

26% **Visit nearby cities**

4% **Take no vacations**

Farming

Above: Handpicking the finest Chinese tea in Hangzhou, Zhejiang Province.

Between 1953 and 1983 the Chinese population doubled. It is now more than 1.5 billion. Between 1980 and 1991 the population was increasing by 1.5 percent per year. As a result China had an additional 17 million mouths to feed every year. Yet grazing land occupies only 16 percent and cultivated land only 14 percent of the country. This is an enormous problem. China is a developing nation and agriculture is not mechanized. The population increase alone absorbs all the annual increase in production.

China's solution to this problem has been intensive farming. Every available piece of arable land is cultivated. Using high-yield varieties of seed, two and three crops are produced in each growing season. Some strains of wheat have been developed which will grow in winter. Terracing makes it possible to grow crops on uneven land and on hillsides. Terraces are now a feature of the landscape throughout China as they are elsewhere in the countries of southeast Asia.

Right: Water buffalo are the most commonly used working animals on the land in China.

Left: Grain is usually threshed manually. This team also has a threshing machine.
Below: A duck farm near Beijing.

Above: Tame cormorants are used on the Li Jiang to dive for fish. They are prevented from swallowing them by a band around the neck.

Wheat is the principal crop of northern China. Rice is the most important in the south. About 400 million tons of grain are produced each year. Other crops suited to conditions in the north include millet, maize, soybeans, tobacco and cotton. The south produces most of China's tea, sugar cane and fruit.

Most peasant families own a pig or a few chickens or ducks. Pork, poultry and eggs produced by peasants make up about a sixth of China's agricultural output.

From the 1950s, the Communist government set up large cooperative farms, where farm workers produced food to sell to government agencies. In the late 1970s, the government introduced reforms, enabling the Chinese to go back to family farming. This led to great increases in farm production.

The Chinese are not great eaters of seafood. Most people live far from the coast. However, more freshwater fish are caught and eaten in China than in any other country.

Resources and industry

China was the first country ever to mine coal and use it as a source of energy. Today China is the world's third largest producer after the United States and the former Soviet Union. Coal provides over 70 percent of China's energy needs. The barren wastelands of the northwest, so unsuited to agriculture, conceal enormous reserves of oil. Like much of China's vast mineral wealth this oil is in sparsely populated and remote regions. Extraction and transportation to refineries is expensive, but new offshore oil fields are being developed with the help of foreign oil companies. China is now self-sufficient in both coal and oil. It has begun to export high-grade petroleum products such as paraffin wax, medical vaseline and industrial lubricants.

China has large deposits of bauxite, uranium, tungsten and low-grade iron ore. With the exception of high-grade iron ore, which it imports for steelmaking, China is completely self-sufficient in energy and exports its surplus minerals to other developing countries.

Above: On board a test rig in the Yellow Sea where British Petroleum is drilling for oil.

Below: Bottles, jars and drinking glasses are made at this factory in Dalian, in Liaoning Province.

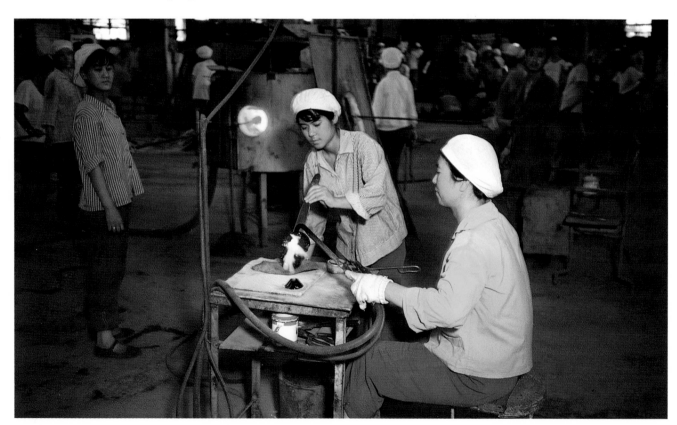

Left: A construction site in the Special Economic Zone of Zhuhi.

Below: Handwoven Chinese cotton and silk carpets are world famous.

Chinese industry is outdated and under-developed. The government has started an ambitious modernization program with the help of loans from the World Bank. Know-how, technology and even fully equipped factories have been imported from western Europe, Japan and Hong Kong.

For many years after the revolution of 1949, most Chinese still lived in poverty. However, earnings and living standards have recently risen steeply and so has the demand for consumer goods. In 1989 Chinese factories produced 27 million television sets, 37 million bicycles, 8 million washing machines and 6 million household refrigerators.

The rapid expansion of consumer goods industries, many of which were financed and run jointly by Chinese and foreign companies, indicates the success of the reforms introduced in the 1980s under the "Four Modernizations" policy. The fastest growing industrial regions are the special economic zones in the east.

Transportation

The pace of life in China is unhurried. There are no high-speed trains or motorways. Only a few roads are surfaced with asphalt. Most roads are little more than dirt tracks linking market villages and farming settlements. But 90 percent of rural communities can now be reached by public bus services as a skeleton trunk road system nears completion.

There are almost no privately owned cars. Until recently owning a car was not allowed. Restrictions have been eased, but cars are still impossibly expensive in China. The trunk roads are needed not for private motorists, but for Chinese industry which until now has had to rely almost solely on the slow and overburdened railroad system for transporting raw materials and finished goods throughout the country.

China has many important navigable inland waterways. The Chang Jiang (formerly Yangzi River) links the major industrial cities of Chongqing, Wuhan and Nanjing.

Above: Despite the poor road network, bus services link all major towns and cities.

Below: Steam, diesel and electric locomotives are all used on China's railway system.

Below: Foreign tourists boarding an aircraft at Guangzhou Airport.

Railroads are the mainstay of the Chinese transportation system. Most trains are pulled by huge black steam locomotives, although there are some diesels and, recently, about 13 percent of the track has been electrified under a policy to extend and improve the rail network. Passengers travel either "hard" or "soft" class. There are also "hard" and "soft" sleeping cars, but the expensive "soft" class is generally occupied by the military, Communist party officials, and foreigners.

The Civil Aviation Administration of China (CAAC) is the supervisory body for several airlines, including Air China, based in Beijing, which has services to 29 countries. Other airlines include China East (based in Shanghai), China South (Guangzhou), China Southwest (Chengdu) and China Northeast (Shenyang). In 1990, 47 airports were able to handle large aircraft, such as Boeing 747s. Besides these American aircraft, the Chinese also use Russian- and British-built aircraft.

Fact file: economy and trade

▽ **The distribution of Chinese economic activity**
Economic activity in China is heavily influenced by the country's climate and physical geography

Industry	
Coal mining	
Oil and gas fields	
Hydroelectric station	

Sheep and goats		Wheat	
Camels		Rice	
Yaks		Cotton	
Pigs		Tea	

Tobacco	
Fruit	
Silk	
Fishing port	

Key Facts

Structure of production: Of the total GDP (the value of all economic activity in China), farming, forestry, and fishing contribute 27 percent, industry 42 percent and services 31 percent. (These are estimates only.)

Farming: Main products: grain, tea, cotton, silk, tobacco, pigs, chickens and horses.

Mining: China is coal rich with reserves of around 900,000 million tons. It also produces tungsten, antimony, nickel, copper, lead and zinc.

Energy: Massive coal, oil and natural gas reserves make

China completely self-sufficient.

Manufacturing: China has chemical, textile, metal and engineering industries.

Economic growth: The average growth rate of China's gross national product (1980-91) was 9.4 percent per year.

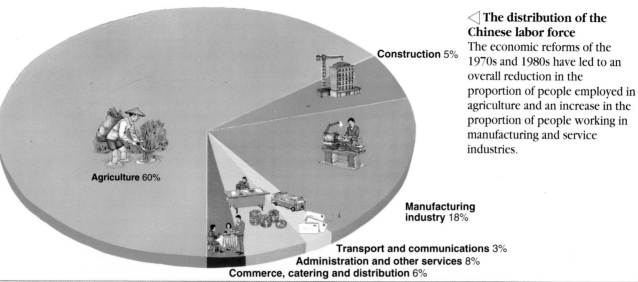

◁ **The distribution of the Chinese labor force**
The economic reforms of the 1970s and 1980s have led to an overall reduction in the proportion of people employed in agriculture and an increase in the proportion of people working in manufacturing and service industries.

Construction 5%

Agriculture 60%

Manufacturing industry 18%

Transport and communications 3%
Administration and other services 8%
Commerce, catering and distribution 6%

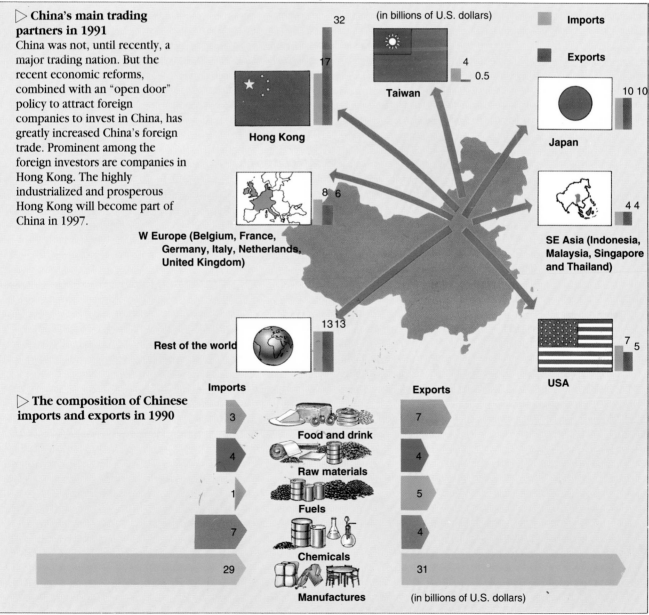

▷ **China's main trading partners in 1991**
China was not, until recently, a major trading nation. But the recent economic reforms, combined with an "open door" policy to attract foreign companies to invest in China, has greatly increased China's foreign trade. Prominent among the foreign investors are companies in Hong Kong. The highly industrialized and prosperous Hong Kong will become part of China in 1997.

(in billions of U.S. dollars)

Imports
Exports

32
17
Hong Kong

Taiwan
4
0.5

Japan
10 10

W Europe (Belgium, France, Germany, Italy, Netherlands, United Kingdom)
8 6

SE Asia (Indonesia, Malaysia, Singapore and Thailand)
4 4

Rest of the world
13 13

USA
7 5

▷ **The composition of Chinese imports and exports in 1990**

Imports
Exports

3 — Food and drink — 7
4 — Raw materials — 4
1 — Fuels — 5
7 — Chemicals — 4
29 — Manufactures — 31

(in billions of U.S. dollars)

Education

Children start school after their sixth birthday. After six years of primary school they can continue at secondary school for a further five years. Although 97 percent of children of school age attend primary school, fewer than half finish secondary school. Many of them begin work at 12 or 14, but continue to attend school part-time. In mountainous and remote regions, where schools are few and poorly equipped, attendance is sporadic. On the high grasslands of Tibet, Xinjiang and Qinghai Provinces, mobile schools enable children to stay with their parents as they follow their flocks in grazing season.

The primary school year lasts nine and a half months. There is a one-month winter vacation and a one-month summer vacation. Older pupils also spend two weeks of social labor planting trees, cleaning classrooms and learning a handicraft. Country schools close during the harvest season so that children can help gather in the crops.

Above: Posters often are used to illustrate the school rules.

Below: A newly built primary school in Xiamen, Fujian Province.

Above: Physical education at a school in Dalian.
Left: Lessons are often chanted aloud and facts learned by heart.

Below: City schools are gradually being equipped with computers as part of China's "Four Modernizations" policy.

Group cooperation is more important than individual achievement in Chinese schools. Pupils have to follow Ministry of Education rules. They are taught to be patriotic, punctual, polite and attentive to teachers and other adults, to be clean, to take regular physical exercise and to be honest and disciplined. Pupils who set the best example can join the Young Pioneers youth organization and wear the highly prized red neckerchief.

All primary school pupils study eight subjects including mathematics, general knowledge and politics. At secondary school there are two special rules for pupils. They are not allowed to drink alcohol or smoke tobacco. And they are strongly encouraged not to fall in love!

School and college dropouts in China do not apply for jobs. The government's Employment Department assigns work to as many as possible. Most people are given jobs at the work unit where they were born. But painful family separations sometimes occur when someone is sent thousands of miles away.

The language

There are more than 1,200 million people throughout the world who speak Chinese – more than twice the number of English speakers. The Chinese language is over 3,000 years old and has been an official language of the United Nations since 1945.

Chinese has no spelling rules, because it has no alphabet. Sentences are built up from over 50,000 "characters" or ideographs which have to be memorized. A typical Chinese twelve-year-old will know about 3,000 characters. Between 4,000 and 6,000 are needed for fluent reading. A highly educated Chinese may be able to use 10,000 characters or more.

The word "ideograph" literally means the drawing of an idea. Most languages began as ideographic, but developed into alphabetic languages. The 26 basic letters of the Roman alphabet represent sounds, not ideas. They can produce millions of words in hundreds of languages. They are also easier to remember than 10,000 Chinese characters.

Above: A young shop assistant practices his calligraphy while he has no customers.

Below: Typing in Chinese is very slow. Characters are selected one at a time.

ㄌㄧㄤ

2840 跟 又讀. 註見 2576.	2849 粱 「高粱」,是穀類植物,為我國北方主要農作物之一.
2841 涼 ①溫度低而不熱叫涼.②當諒字,如「涼德」.	**ㄌㄧㄤˇ(上)**
2842 凉 是「涼」字的俗體.	2850 兩 ①當「雙」字講,如「兩人」,「兩全其美」.②是重量名,十錢叫「一兩」.
2843 輬 「輼輬」,註見 9449.	2851 两 是「兩」字的俗體.
2844 量 ①用升斗秤尺計算東西的多少,長短,輕重叫量,如「量米」,「量布」,「秤量」.②當商酌講,如「商量」.	2852 両 是「兩」字的簡體.
2845 糧 ①穀類食物統叫糧,如「糧食」.②舊時田賦叫「錢糧」.	2853 倆 「伎倆」,註見 4375.
2846 粮 同「糧」字.	2854 魎 「魍魎」,註見 9490.
2847 梁 ①建築房屋架於柱上的橫木叫梁.②是戰國時的國名,又是五代時的朝代名.③「橋梁」,就是橋.④橫暴叫「強梁」.⑤是姓.	2855 蜽 同「魎」字.
	2856 裲 「裲襠」,是只有胸背兩面的衣服.
2848 樑 是「梁」字的俗體.	2857 緉 鞋子一雙叫緉.
	ㄌㄧㄤˋ(去)
	2858 晾 放在通風的地方使乾叫晾,如「晾衣裳」.
	2859 涼 「涼涼」,是把熱的東西晾著使冷的意思.
(一六七)	2840—2861

CHINESE PHOENETIC ALPHABET	PRONOUNCED AS IN		
a	far	n	no
b	be	o	law
c	its	p	par
ch	church	q	cheek
d	do	r	roll
e	her	s	sister
ei	way	sh	shore
f	foot	t	top
g	go	u	too
i	eat or sir	w	want
j	jeep	x	she
k	kind	y	yet
l	land	z	zero
m	me	zh	jump

Left: A page from a chinese dictionary.
Below: Public storytellers still attract large crowds.

Above: *Pinyin* is the official system for writing Chinese in the Roman alphabet.

There are dozens of spoken dialects in Chinese, which are as different from one another as English, German, Danish, and Dutch. About two-thirds of the population speak Mandarin, which is the dialect of Beijing. Mandarin is officially recognized as the *putonghua* – the approved, commonly spoken dialect of the People's Republic of China.

An inhabitant of Beijing will not understand the spoken Chinese of someone from Guangzhou, but they will both understand each other's written Chinese. The characters remain the same because they represent the idea – not the sound – of a word.

Chinese characters are like Arabic numerals. To the French, 2 is *deux*. To the Germans, 2 is *zwei*. The Swedes say *två*, and the Chinese say *er*, but they all understand the symbol 2 in the same way. In Beijing λ is said *ren*. In Guangzhou they say *yan*. In Shanghai it's *nin*. The Japanese say *hitoh*, and the Koreans say *in*. But they all understand λ to mean man.

The arts

The Chinese were probably the first to fire clay at high temperatures to produce ceramics. Cooking and storage pots made in the Neolithic or New Stone Age have been found at Banpo, near Xi'an. By the time of the first Chinese emperor, Shih Huang Di (259-210 B.C.), ceramics were used as burial objects. Over the centuries the techniques of glazing and firing were continuously refined. The magnificent vases of the Ming dynasty (1368-1644) are almost priceless today.

Mao Zedong, the revolutionary leader, believed that every picture, story, play and piece of music should show the people how great China could become under Communism. Enormous posters depicting a modernized and militarily strong China were the most popular art form of the Cultural Revolution (1966-76).

Peasant artists were commissioned to paint realistic scenes of agricultural life with tractors, bumper crops and laborers working happily. Mao exploited the arts to inspire the people with faith in his leadership and hope for the future.

Above: Shih Huang Di's burial army of 7,000 life-size terra cotta figures was unearthed in Lintung, in Shaanxi Province, in 1974.

Below: Designs from 4,000 years ago are now used on souvenir badges.

Left: Delicate paper-cuts made by peasant farm-workers in Sichuan Province.

Above: *The Pig Farm*, a wood-cut by peasant painters at the Huxian Peasant Painting Institute in Shaanxi Province.
Left: The bamboo plant is a constant inspiration to Chinese artists.

Below: Peking Opera is based on ancient stories that almost all Chinese know well. The ancient language in which the operas are sung is not understood by many people.

China's literature, which dates back almost 3,000 years, is rich and varied. The stories of Lu Xun (1881-1936), which have working-class heroes and are critical of the country's old imperial leaders, are very popular in modern China.

Chinese opera has a long and distinguished history, but it is almost unknown outside China. There are over 100 regional variations, but the best-known is "Peking Opera." No stage props or scenery are used and it is sung in a high-pitched ancient Chinese.

Calligraphy – or handwriting with a brush – developed as an art form over 2,000 years ago. The artistic qualities of handwritten Chinese characters can reflect what the characters mean.

The paper-cut is a popular and well-known Chinese art form. Traditional designs are cut into thin tissue paper with a sharp blade and are used to decorate people's homes on special occasions.

The making of modern China

On October 1, 1949, in the heart of Beijing, the Communist Party's leader, Chairman Mao Zedong, proclaimed the People's Republic of China.

Two thousand years earlier, the emperor Qin (from whose name we get the word China) had been the first to unify the numerous states and provinces into one nation. From the time of Qin until the beginning of the 20th century, a succession of immensely rich and powerful imperial families or dynasties ruled China. Over 90 percent of the people were illiterate peasants living in extreme poverty.

During the 17th century Portugal, the Netherlands and Britain began to develop their overseas empires. They became increasingly interested in trade with China. Britain wanted to trade its cheap cloth for China's tea and silk. The Chinese emperors had long regarded China as the center of the civilized world. The Chinese word for China is *Zhong-guo* meaning "middle kingdom." Foreigners were barbarian upstarts, to be ignored and kept out.

Above: A wealthy Shanghai merchant with his child servants during the 1890s.
Below: This family in Hunan Province lived in this hole (about 1920).

Right: Dr Sun Yat Sen (1866-1925) was the leader of the Guomindang and became the first president of the Republic of China in 1912.

The British crippled China's economy by flooding the country with Indian opium for which addicts had to pay in silver. In 1842 the Chinese surrendered Hong Kong to the British.

Foreign domination, weak government and the extreme poverty of the people were the causes of a series of revolutions and civil wars. In 1911 a republican government led by Dr. Sun Yat Sen, replaced the monarchy.

Of all the newly formed political parties in 20th-century China, only the Communists had a policy of land reform. After Sun Yat Sen's death The National People's Party (Guomindang) mercilessly persecuted the Communists, who in 1934 had to flee to the north. Chairman Mao led his Red Army 6,000 miles (9,600 km) through 11 provinces on the "Long March." Thousands died on the way but the Communists gained the respect and support of the people. After World War II Mao took control of the country. In 1949, the Guomindang was forced into exile in Taiwan.

Above: The revolutionary leader Mao Zedong (1893-1976) on the "Long March."

Below: Mao became the head of state in 1949 and held the position until his death in 1976.

China in the modern world

Once in power the Communists confiscated all privately owned land. Many landlords were sentenced to death and land was redistributed to the peasants. Eventually people's communes and collective farms were established. China's economy was planned in five-year cycles. Heavy industry began to develop for the first time.

In the 1960s several politicians attempted to replace Mao as leader. In 1966 he launched the Cultural Revolution to strengthen his own position.

The Cultural Revolution was a ten-year disaster for China. Mao inspired millions of teenagers to become Red Guards. They roamed the cities and the countryside in large groups vandalizing property and beating up anyone they suspected of not supporting Mao. Schools and universities were favorite targets. Teachers were publicly humiliated, tortured and often murdered. No one in the country felt secure during the Cultural Revolution. Finally in 1976 the army had to restore order.

Above: A red book containing the thoughts of Mao was carried by everybody during the Cultural Revolution.
Below: People wore large badges made of metal or porcelain to show their support for Mao during the Cultural Revolution.

Left: Large posters encourage couples to have only one child.

Left: In May 1989 students in Beijing put up a statue of the "Goddess of Democracy," modeled on the Statue of Liberty.
Below: Chris Patten, the last governor of Hong Kong, reviews the guard in 1992.

Above: Hong Kong, one of the world's leading financial centers, will return to Chinese rule in 1997, after 155 years as a British Crown Colony.

Mao Zedong died on September 9, 1976. He had been a great military leader, but he made many political mistakes toward the end of his life. China is still paying for some of them. A whole generation of school and university students remained uneducated during the Cultural Revolution.

China is now a world power, though it faces many problems. Today's priorities for Chinese leaders include population control and the "Four Modernizations" policy. This policy is aimed at four areas: agriculture, defense, industry, and science and technology.

Some Chinese talk of a "Fifth Modernization." By this, they mean the reform of government and the introduction of democracy. Large student demonstrations calling for democracy were held in Tiananmen Square, Beijing, and also in other cities in 1989. But China's Communist leaders declared their opposition to political reforms and ordered troops to break up the demonstrations and arrest the student leaders.

Fact file: government and world role

Key Facts

Official name: People's Republic of China.

Flag: One large and four small yellow stars (to symbolize the unity of the people – peasants, workers, soldiers and students – under the Communist Party) on a red background (to symbolize the spirit of the revolution that led to the founding of the People's Republic on October 1, 1949).

National emblem: Shows Tiananmen (Gate of Heavenly Peace) in Beijing, lit by the five stars and encircled with ears of wheat (representing agriculture). A cogwheel represents industry.

National anthem: *March of the Volunteers* (words by Tien Han; music by Nie Er, 1935).

National Government: *Head of State:* The President of the People's Congress Standing Committee of the National Government

Legislature: State Council of the National People's Congress. Theoretically the National Government may be independent of the Communist Party. In practice the President and Members of the Standing Committee of the National People's Congress are also General Secretary, President, Vice-President, Chairman and Members of the Communist Party's Central Committee and Politburo.

Armed forces (1991): There are 2.3 million people in China's land forces and a further 12 million in para-military (civilian) forces. The air force has 470,000 men and women and the navy about 240,000.

Membership: China is a member of the U.N. and one of the five members of the U.N. Security Council. China belongs to the International Monetary Fund and the Asian Development Bank.

▽ **The regions of China**

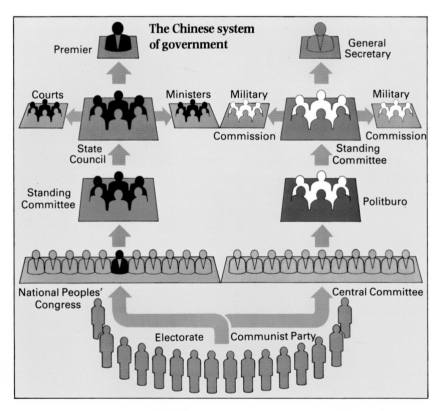

The Chinese system of government

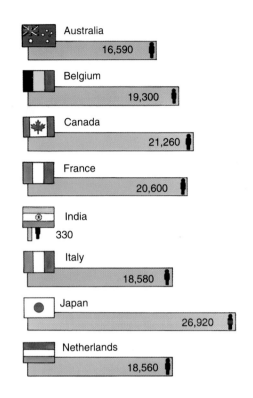

Country	Wealth
Australia	16,590
Belgium	19,300
Canada	21,260
France	20,600
India	330
Italy	18,580
Japan	26,920
Netherlands	18,560

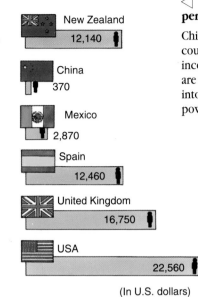

Country	Wealth
New Zealand	12,140
China	370
Mexico	2,870
Spain	12,460
United Kingdom	16,750
USA	22,560

(In U.S. dollars)

◁ **National wealth created per person in 1991**

China is among the poorer countries of the world, in terms of income per person. Great efforts are being made to transform China into a modern developed economic power.

▽ **The Chinese influence**
Over the centuries Chinese have emigrated to all the countries of southeast Asia. People with Chinese origins form a large part of the population in Hong Kong (1), Taiwan (2), Singapore (3), Thailand (4), The Philippines (5), Malaysia (6) and Indonesia (7). Cities in other countries, with significant Chinese communities include Sydney (8), London (9), New York (10), Los Angeles (11) and San Francisco (12).

Index